D038217

MAY   2004

ATTACK FIGHTERS

IAN GRAHAM

Heinemann Library
Chicago, Illinois

Customer Service 888-454-2279
Visit our website at www.heinemannlibrary.com

Designed by Jo Hinton-Malivoire and Tinstar Design Limited (www.tinstar.co.uk)
Illustrations by Geoff Ward
Originated by Dot Gradations Ltd
Printed and bound in Hong Kong, China by South China Printing

07 06 05 04 03
10 9 8 7 6 5 4 3 2 1

Library of Congress Cataloging-in-Publication Data
Graham, Ian, 1953-
  Attack fighters / Ian Graham.
      p. cm. -- (Designed for success)
Summary: Provides an overview of the design and engineering of the jet planes that are designed to attack other aircraft.
Includes bibliographical references and index.
  ISBN 1-40340-769-X (Library Binding - hardcover)
  1. Fighter planes--Juvenile literature. [1. Fighter planes. 2. Airplanes, Military.] I. Title. II. Series.
  UG1242.F5 G675 2002
  623.7'464--dc21
                        2002006072
Acknowledgments
The author and publishers are grateful to the following for permission to reproduce copyright material: pp. 1, 9 (top), 15 (top), 18 EPA; pp. 3, 27 (bottom) Flight Collection/Erik Simonsen; p. 4 (top and bottom) TRH Pictures/Douglas McDonnell; pp. 5 (top), 11, 16 Aviation Picture Library; p. 5 (bottom) TRH Pictures/Paul Reynolds; pp. 6, 9 (bottom), 13 (bottom), 23, 27 (top) TRH Pictures; p. 7 (top) TRH Pictures/Peter Modigh; p. 10 (top) Corbis/Roger Ressmeyer; p. 10 (bottom) Flight Collection/Mark Wagner; pp. 12 (top), 13 (top) Defense Visual Information Center; p. 14 TRH Pictures/Lockheed Martin; pp. 15 (bottom), 20, 21 (top) Corbis; p. 17 (top and bottom) Pratt & Whitney; p. 17 (middle) TRH Pictures/Peter Holman; pp. 19 (top and bottom), 28 Flight Collection; pp. 22, 24 Skyscan Photo Library/Chris Allan; p. 25 (top) API; p. 25 (middle) TRH Pictures/Macdonald; p. 25 (bottom) MPL; p. 26 Aviation Picture Library/Austin J. Brown; p. 29 TRH Pictures/US National Archives.

Cover photograph reproduced with permission of Corbis (plane) and Getty Images (background).

Our thanks to Captain Barton Buchanan for his comments in the preparation of this book.

Every effort has been made to contact copyright holders of any material reproduced in this book. Any omissions will be rectified in subsequent printings if notice is given to the publishers.

Some words are shown in bold, **like this.** You can find out what they mean by looking in the glossary.

CONTENTS

Attack Fighters 4

Designing Fighters 6

Stealth Attack .8

Closer Look: Lockheed F-22 Raptor . . .10

Engine Power 16

Navy Fighters 18

Jump Jets 20

Fly-By-Wire 22

Safety First 24

Fast and Furious 26

Data Files 28

Further Reading 29

Glossary 30

Index 32

ATTACK FIGHTERS

Fighters are small, fast, well-armed jet airplanes. They are designed to attack other aircraft. New fighters are being developed all the time to make them better and better.

The American F-15 Eagle set new standards for modern fighters when it was designed in the 1960s. It flew for the first time in 1972. Its speed and **maneuverability** meant it could outfly any other fighter in the world. The F-15 is a type of aircraft called an **air-superiority fighter.** Its job is to clear the sky of enemy airplanes. Fighters often do other work, too. Fighter-bombers and strike fighters can attack targets on the ground.

AIR-TO-AIR COMBAT

The F-15 attacks other airplanes with a cannon, which is a type of aircraft machine gun, and up to eight missiles. The cannon can fire up to 100 **rounds** a minute. The missiles are carried under the wings and body. The missiles can be a mixture of:

- AIM-7 Sparrows
- AIM-9 Sidewinders
- AIM-120 AMRAAMs (Advanced Medium-Range Air-to-Air Missiles).

STRIKE EAGLE

The F-15 can work as an **interceptor.** It can fly a long distance at top speed to meet incoming fighters or bombers and stop them. It was so successful that a new type of F-15 was developed that could also attack targets on the ground. This version is called the F-15E Strike Eagle.

SINGLE-SEATER

The F-15 was originally going to have a crew of two. However, the design was changed to enable one pilot to fly it. All the switches that controlled the weapons were fitted to the control **stick.** This enabled the pilot to fire the airplane's weapons without taking his or her hands off the flight controls. The second crewperson, the weapons officer, was no longer needed. So, the F-15 became a single-seater.

When the F-15E Strike Eagle fighter-bomber was developed, the airplane's weapons became even more complicated. The pilot could no longer do everything unaided. So, a second seat and **cockpit** were installed behind the pilot for a weapons officer.

IN-FLIGHT REFUELING

An F-15E can be refueled without landing. A tanker-airplane has a hose trailing behind it. The end plugs into a socket on the left side of the F-15E. Fuel flows from the tanker into the F-15E's tanks. In-flight refueling means that an F-15E can fly as long or as far as it needs to. It is not limited by the size of its fuel tanks.

F-15E Strike Eagle

Type: strike fighter-bomber
Country: United States
Crew: 2
Wingspan: 43 ft (13.1 m)
Top speed: 1,650 mph (2,655km/hr)
Max weight: 80,997 lb (36,740 kg)
Weapon load: 24,493 lb (11,110 kg)

DESIGNING FIGHTERS

The design of a fighter depends on the job it has to do. Designers try to produce fighters that outperform any enemy aircraft and other defenses they might encounter.

Fighters have to be able to chase enemy airplanes and also escape from airplanes that attack them. Being able to turn very tightly helps them do this and win air battles called dogfights. A superfast top speed is not so important for dogfighting because slower airplanes can turn more tightly. However, some fighters that are designed to do other jobs are very fast. **Interceptors** have a very high top speed so that they can reach approaching enemy airplanes as quickly as possible when they are still far away from their targets. Most can fly twice the speed of sound. A few, including the Russian MiG-25 and MiG-31, can top three times the speed of sound. That is more than 1,900 mph (3,000 km/hr)!

JOINING FORCES

As its name suggests, the Eurofighter is a fighter built by a group of European airplane makers. Britain, Spain, Germany, and Italy shared the work and the huge cost of developing the new fighter. France was involved at the beginning but left to develop its own fighter called Rafale. Eurofighter is an **air-superiority fighter** designed to do the same job as the F-15.

GRIPEN

The Saab Gripen is a Swedish multi-role fighter. It is designed to fly three different types of missions:

- It can fight other aircraft.
- It can attack targets on the ground.
- It can spy on the enemy, which is called reconnaissance.

The Gripen can be prepared for a new mission by only five people and within just ten minutes of landing!

This Gripen is on a mission over the snow-covered terrain of northern Sweden.

Control surfaces

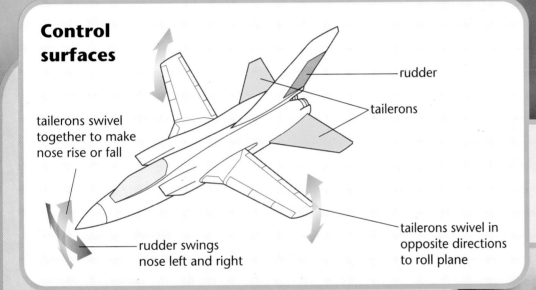

rudder

tailerons

tailerons swivel together to make nose rise or fall

rudder swings nose left and right

tailerons swivel in opposite directions to roll plane

This illustration shows an aircraft that is controlled using tailerons.

STEERING AIRPLANES

A pilot steers by moving parts of an airplane's wings and tail called **control surfaces.** When the **rudder** or the **tail fin** swivels to one side, air rushing past the airplane hits it and swings the tail around. Swiveling the **elevators** or the **tailplanes** causes the airplane to climb or dive. **Ailerons** in the wings swivel in opposite directions, making the airplane roll. Sometimes one part does two jobs. Tailplanes that also do the ailerons' job are called tailerons. Wing flaps that work as ailerons are called flaperons. And ailerons that also do the elevators' job are called elevons.

Eurofighter EFA 2000

Type: multirole fighter
Country: UK/Germany/Italy/Spain
Crew: 1
Wingspan: 34.5 ft (10.5 m)
Top speed: 1,320 mph (2,125 km/hr)
Max weight: 42,297 lb (21,000 kg)
Weapon load: 14,330 lb (6,500 kg)

STEALTH ATTACK

Aircraft can be detected by **radar** long before they can be seen. This makes it very difficult for attack airplanes to surprise their enemies.

One solution to this problem is to fly close to the ground or behind hills or mountains, where radar does not work well. This is called terrain masking. However, low flying is very dangerous. Airplanes risk crashing into hills or being hit by missiles or gunfire from the ground. Another solution is to design an airplane that cannot be found by radar. If the airplane is exactly the right shape and covered with the right materials, it disappears from radar screens. An aircraft designed to do this is called a stealth airplane. The Lockheed F-117 Nighthawk is one example of a stealth airplane. Its body is designed to **disperse** radar waves so that they cannot be detected. The airplane is also coated with radar-absorbing materials.

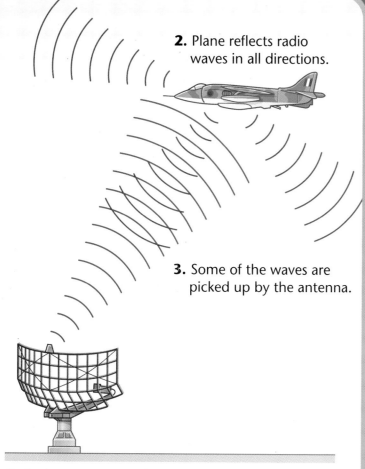

2. Plane reflects radio waves in all directions.

3. Some of the waves are picked up by the antenna.

1. Radar antenna sends out bursts of radio waves.

RADAR

Radar finds aircraft by sending out radio waves and picking up any waves that are reflected back. It's like throwing a ball. If it bounces back, you know there is something in front of you. The time it takes for the ball to bounce back tells you how far away it is. Radar works faster than a bouncing ball because radio waves travel at the speed of light—186,000 miles (300,000 kilometers) per second!

Lockheed F-117 Nighthawk

Type: stealth attack aircraft

Country: United States

Crew: 1

Wingspan: 43.3 ft (13.2 m)

Top speed: 610 mph (980 km/hr)

Max weight: 52,503 lb (23,815 kg)

Weapon load: 5,005 lb (2,270 kg)

engines

This Nighthawk has just landed. The parachute is used to slow the plane down.

CARRYING WEAPONS

Attack airplanes often hang their weapons underneath their wings and bodies. The shape of its weapons makes it easier to detect an airplane using radar. The Nighthawk carries its weapons inside its body, so they do not spoil its carefully designed shape. As the airplane approaches its target, doors in the bottom of its body open and the weapons are released.

HIDING ENGINES

A fighter's engines are very difficult to hide from an enemy. Their heat and spinning blades can be detected from very far away. The Nighthawk's engines are buried deep inside its wings, so they are more difficult to detect. And the hot **exhaust** from its engines is mixed with cold air to cool them down.

JAGGED EDGE

Every part of the Nighthawk is designed to keep it from being detected by radar. Even the edge of the **cockpit** canopy that closes over the pilot is specially designed. It has a jagged edge, as this is more difficult for radar to spot than a straight edge.

LOCKHEED F-22 RAPTOR
TESTING TIMES

In the 1980s, the U.S. Air Force decided to begin developing a new fighter to replace its F-15. The U.S. government then asked seven U.S. airplane-makers to produce designs.

Two designs, from Lockheed and Northrop, went on to the next stage of the competition. This involved building and testing the two competing aircraft. The Lockheed design won and became the F-22 Raptor. The F-22 is a twin-engine jet airplane designed to be more powerful and more **maneuverable** than any existing fighter. The shape of its wings and **fuselage** were carefully designed to make the airplane hard to find by **radar.** The pilot sits high up because this gives a clear view all around the airplane.

COMPUTER TESTING

Using computers for design and testing saves time and cuts costs. It is called virtual product development. A copy of the airplane is created in a computer system. The computer runs tests called **simulations.** The tests show any parts that don't fit or work correctly. These problems are dealt with quickly on the computer screen before any real parts are made. These tests used to be done by building models and full-size aircraft.

FLYING TEST BED

Parts of the F-22 were fitted to a Boeing 757 airline so they could be tested before the airplane was built. An F-22 **cockpit** was built inside the airplane and an F-22 nose was built on the front. An extra wing was added on top. Sensors in the wing were connected to the F-22 instruments and computers. Company scientists and engineers checked how well they worked.

SWIVELING JETS

The F-22 can do something that most fighters cannot do. The **exhaust** nozzles at the back of its engines will swivel up or down when the pilot moves the controls. This is called vectored **thrust** and makes the airplane more maneuverable. When both nozzles point upward, the nose rises, and the airplane climbs. When both nozzles swivel down, the nose is lowered, and the airplane dives. When one points up and the other down, the airplane rolls.

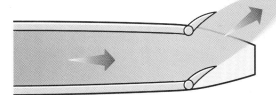

When both nozzles point upward, the tail of the F-22 is forced down, and the airplane climbs.

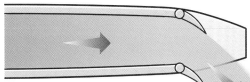

When both nozzles point downward, the tail is forced up, and the airplane dives.

The YF-22 was flight-tested at all speeds, heights, and angles— even straight up in the air!

THE FIRST F-22

Lockheed's prototype, or test model, for the F-22 was called the YF-22. It flew for the first time in 1990. A series of test flights proved that it could do everything the computer simulations predicted it could. The results of the test flights enabled the designers to fine-tune its shape. They made the **tail fins** smaller and the nose blunter. Then manufacturing could begin.

LOCKHEED F-22 RAPTOR

Here the F-22's electronic equipment is being tested by an engineer sitting in the **cockpit.**

Most fighters are built from aluminum and steel, but the F-22 is different. Its performance depends on the use of different materials.

Most of the F-22 is made from **titanium** and composites. A composite is made from two different materials, which are stronger together than they are separately. Titanium and composites were chosen because they are strong and lightweight and can withstand high temperatures. The airplane's main frame is made mostly from titanium. The rest of the airplane is built onto this frame. The composite parts are made by laying flexible sheets of composite material on top of each other in a mold. The fabriclike material is then soaked in a liquid plastic called resin. Finally, the part is cooked in a special oven to harden the resin.

Who makes what?

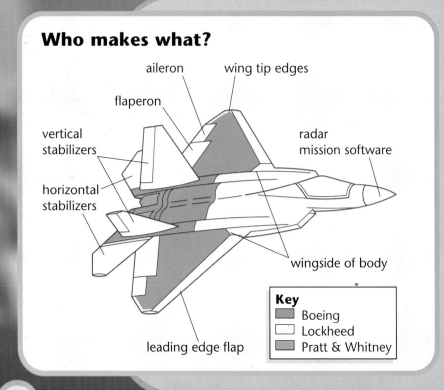

aileron
wing tip edges
flaperon
vertical stabilizers
radar mission software
horizontal stabilizers
wingside of body
leading edge flap

Key
- Boeing
- Lockheed
- Pratt & Whitney

JOINT EFFORT

Building a fighter is a large and complicated project. It requires so many different skills that several manufacturers work together. The main structure of the F-22 is made by two companies—Boeing and Lockheed Martin. Boeing makes the wings and tail end of the **fuselage.** Lockheed Martin makes the rest of the **airframe.** Pratt & Whitney supplies the engines. Hundreds of other companies supply the computers, instruments, and other equipment inside the aircraft.

FLIGHT COMPUTER

The F-22 is fitted with some of the most advanced avionics, or aviation electronics, ever put in an aircraft. It includes a powerful computer to bring all the information from its systems together and present it clearly to the pilot. The F-22's main computer works 100,000 times faster than the computer used in the Apollo Lunar Module that landed the first astronauts on the moon. It also stores 8,000 times as much information.

The F-22's computer might look simple, but it is the world's most advanced high-speed computer system for use in an attack fighter.

COMPUTERIZED COCKPIT

An F-22 pilot sits in front of a bank of computer screens. However, in **combat** the pilot is too busy to look down at them. The most important information is projected onto a glass screen called a Head-Up Display (HUD) in front of the pilot.

F-22 Raptor

Type: advanced tactical fighter
Country: United States
Crew: 1
Wingspan: 44.3 ft (13.5 m)
Top speed: 1,245 mph (over 2,000 km/hr)
Max weight: 59,999 lb (27,215 kg)
Weapon load: classified

"It [the F-22] is not an airplane you use to defend your airspace. It's an airplane that is used to dominate the other guy's airspace."
General Ronald R. Fogleman, former Chief of Staff, U.S. Air Force

LOCKHEED F-22 RAPTOR

FAST AND FURIOUS

The F-22 Raptor has an amazing flight performance. It can fly as slow as a small propeller airplane or as fast as a **supersonic interceptor.**

Airplanes designed to fly at twice the speed of sound are usually very bad at flying slowly. They are the wrong shape. Their wings are designed to work best when they are flying at more than 1,245 mph (2,000 kph). Amazingly, the F-22 can fly as slowly as a Piper Cub, a small single-engine propeller airplane with a top speed of only 85 mph (140 kph). Then it can boost its engines to full power and accelerate to more than **Mach** 2, twice the speed of sound. The F-22 is expected to be in military service by 2005.

KEEPING COOL

Fighter pilots work very hard and have to wear a lot of safety clothing while flying. This means they become very hot. So, F-22 pilots have a special cooling layer in their suits. Cool air pumped through this layer carries unwanted heat away from the pilot's body.

INFORMATION OVERLOAD

The pilots of modern fighters are kept busy just making sense of all the information flooding into the **cockpit.** The F-22's computers sort through it all and show the pilot only the most important information. Several F-22s flying together can also exchange information among their computers automatically, without the pilots having to say a word.

CRAZY ANGLES

The F-22 is designed to be the most agile fighter of all. The pilot can make the airplane turn fast enough at all speeds to be able to point and shoot at enemy aircraft. The combination of vectored **thrust** and advanced flight controls enables the F-22 to turn and shoot faster than any aircraft it will ever have to face in **combat.**

Ernst Mach, around 1890

MACH NUMBERS

The speed of sound is also called Mach 1. Mach numbers are named after scientist Ernst Mach, who was interested in what happens to air when something moves through it very quickly. The speed of sound is different in different places. Near the ground, where the air is warm, sound travels at about 760 mph (1,225 km/hr). Higher up, where the air is much colder, the speed of sound falls to about 620 mph (1,000 km/hr).

ENGINE POWER

Fighters are powered by **jet engines.** Small, lightweight fighters have one engine. Larger, long-range fighters and heavier fighter-bombers have two engines.

A fan at the front of the engine sucks in air. The air passes through a device called a compressor. There the air is squashed before fuel is sprayed into the compressor and burned. This heats the air to more than 2,732°F (1,500°C). This is hot enough to melt iron! Hot air takes up more space than cold air does. As the air inside the engine expands, it has to go somewhere. It cannot go forward because more air is constantly being forced into the engine. So it escapes through the back of the engine as powerful **exhaust** that thrusts the aircraft forward. On its way, it spins a **turbine** that drives the fan and compressor.

AIR POWER

A jet engine produces its enormous power simply by heating air. This illustration of a Pratt & Whitney F-119-PW-100 engine shows how the process works.

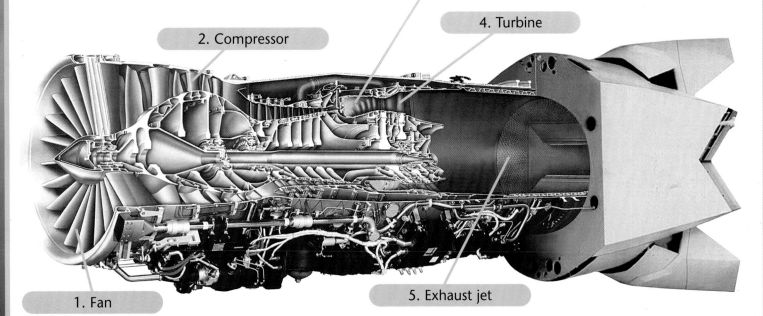

1. Fan sucks in cold air.
2. Compressor squashes air.
3. Fuel is burned inside the combustion chamber.
4. Turbine spins and drives the fan and compressor.
5. Air leaves the engine as hot, fast exhaust.

3. Combustion chamber

2. Compressor

4. Turbine

1. Fan

5. Exhaust jet

POWERING THE F-22

The F-22 Raptor is powered by two Pratt & Whitney F-119-PW-100 jet engines. They were specially designed for the F-22. They are twice as powerful as any other fighter engine when the airplane is flying faster than sound. The engine was designed with advice from those who would build it and repair it. The result was an engine that is easier to build and quicker to repair than most fighter engines.

EUROFIGHTER'S ENGINES

The Eurofighter is powered by two EJ-200 jet engines. The EJ-200 is roughly the same size as the engine that powers the older Tornado fighter-bomber that the Eurofighter will replace. However, the EJ-200 has 1,000 fewer parts and is 50 percent more powerful than the Tornado engine. Designers try to build engines with fewer parts because simpler engines are more reliable.

This F-22 is using its afterburners. You can see the flames where the fuel has ignited.

BOOSTING POWER

A fighter engine can be made more powerful with an afterburner. An afterburner sprays fuel into the hot exhaust that comes from the engine. The fuel burns and gives the airplane an extra push. Afterburners can help heavy airplanes take off or give an extra burst of speed in **combat**. The F-22 is the only fighter than can fly faster than sound for long periods without using an afterburner. This is called supercruise.

NAVY FIGHTERS

The world's largest navies and marine forces have their own fighter airplanes. These aircraft are specially designed or modified for service on ships.

U.S. Navy fighters such as the F-14 Tomcat and F/A-18 Hornet have to withstand the most demanding conditions of any **combat** aircraft. They are based on ships called aircraft carriers that have a runway on their decks. Navy pilots land their airplanes by slamming them down hard onto the carrier's deck. A hook in the airplane's tail catches a cable strung across the deck and stops the airplane. The airplane's landing gear has to be made extra strong to survive these jarring landings, which are more like controlled crashes. Takeoffs are hard on navy fighters, too. A **catapult** connected to the airplane's **nosewheel** launches it along the deck. Within 3 seconds, it is airborne and going 155 mph (250 km/hr).

TOMCAT

A fully laden and fueled F-14 Tomcat can weigh up to 32 tons at takeoff. That is as much as twenty small family cars. It works as a **supersonic interceptor** and also as a fighter-bomber carrying heavy weapons. It handles these different demands by having wings that can move. It is called a swing-wing design, or **variable geometry.** For takeoff and landing, its wings stick straight out from the sides. This is the best position for flying slowly.

SWINGING WINGS

Once the Tomcat is in the air, its wings automatically swing backward to suit its speed. As it flies faster, the wings move back farther. At its top speed of about 1,555 mph (2,500 km/hr), its wings and tail form a triangular, or delta, shape. This is the best shape for supersonic flight.

Here the Tomcat has its wings swept back in a delta shape.

F-14 Tomcat

Type: navy interceptor/fighter-bomber
Country: United States
Crew: 2
Wingspan: 64 ft (19.5 m) (max)
Top speed: 1,555 mph (2,500 km/hr)
Max weight: 70,768 lb (32,100 kg)
Weapon load: 14,506 lb (6,580 kg)

FOLDING TIPS

When an F/A-18 Hornet lands on a carrier's deck, its wing tips begin to fold up. Folding wings make it possible to park airplanes closer together, so more airplanes can fit into the limited space onboard ship. As a Hornet **taxies** to the end of the flight deck for a new mission, its wing tips unfold again and lock into position, ready for takeoff.

JUMP JETS

Nearly all fighters have to move along the ground at high speed before their wings can lift them into the air. Jump jet fighters can fly in a different way.

Jump jets can take off vertically, as helicopters do. They do this by pointing the **thrust** from their engine downward to push the airplane upward. The engine, not the wings, produces **lift.** Then the jets are swiveled backward, and the airplane flies off in the normal way. Jump jets can be based almost anywhere because they don't need a runway. This makes it more difficult for enemies to find and attack them. Vertical takeoff uses so much fuel that jump jets often use a short takeoff run to help them get into the air. This way of using the airplane is called short takeoff and vertical landing (STOVL).

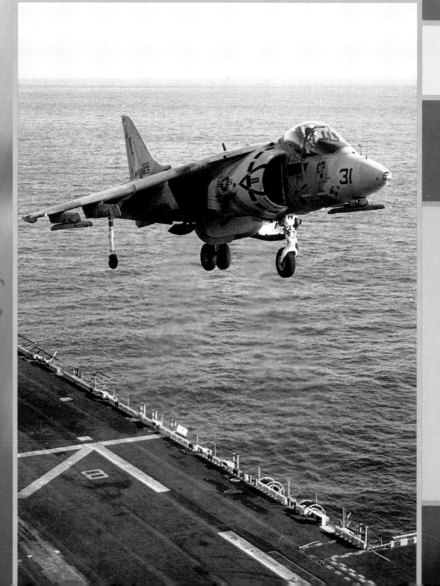

A Harrier takes off from the flight deck of the USS *Saipan* aircraft carrier.

HARRIER II

The first practical jump jet, and the most successful, is the Harrier. The latest model, the Harrier II, is often stationed aboard ships that also carry helicopters. It may take off from a ski jump at the end of the ship's deck. The ski jump tips the airplane's nose upward at the end of its takeoff run.

A SPECIAL ENGINE

The Harrier needs a special engine for its special flying abilities. A **jet engine** usually produces one jet, or stream, of gas that comes straight out of the back of the engine. The Harrier's Pegasus engine produces four jets—two at the front and two at the back. To take off vertically, the pilot turns the four engine nozzles so that they point downward. The four jets push the airplane straight up in the air. To fly forward, the pilot turns the nozzles to point backward.

HOVERING

A pilot usually steers an airplane by moving parts of the wings and tail. This works only when the airplane is moving quickly through the air. When a jump jet hovers or takes off vertically, it doesn't move quickly enough to be steered this way. Instead, small jets of air from the engine are blown from the nose, wing tips, and tail to control the airplane's position.

Harrier II

Type: STOVL close support aircraft
Country: UK/U.S.
Crew: 1
Wingspan: 30.5 ft (9.3 m)
Top speed: 660 mph (1,065 km/hr)
Max weight: 30,997 lb (14,060 kg)
Weapon load: 13,228 lb (6,000 kg)

Control while hovering

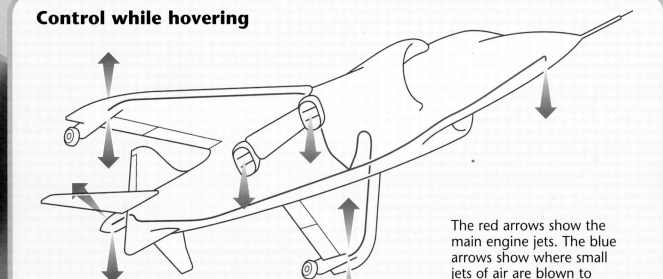

The red arrows show the main engine jets. The blue arrows show where small jets of air are blown to control the airplane's position while hovering.

FLY-BY-WIRE

Modern fighters are flown with the help of computers. Using computers to control airplanes in flight has made it possible to design a new type of fighter.

A fighter pilot steers by moving a **stick** similar to a video game joystick. When the stick moves, computers sense the movement and make the airplane do what the pilot wants it to do. It is called fly-by-wire because the controls are connected to the airplane's computers by electrical wires. Most airplanes fly straight and level if the pilot lets go of the controls. They are said to be stable. The latest fighters are not stable. They would tumble end over end unless their position was corrected every fraction of a second. Their flight computers take care of this vital task automatically. The advantage of making a fighter unstable is that when the pilot wants it to turn, it turns instantly. Making a fighter more **maneuverable** in this way means it is more likely to survive an air battle.

FIGHTING FALCON

The F-16 Fighting Falcon was one of the first fly-by-wire fighters. It made its first flight in 1974. It can make amazingly tight turns. The pilot can be forced down into his or her seat so hard in a turn that his or her body weight feels up to nine times greater than normal. This is called **G-force.** The pilot's arms feel so heavy that it is hard to keep hold of the controls, or even to breathe. However, the F-16 has been so successful that more of them are flown by **Western** air forces than any other fighter.

BACKSEAT DRIVERS

When a new single-seat fighter like the F-16 is produced, a small number of them are built with two seats in the **cockpit** instead of one. The second seat is used to give experienced fighter pilots their final training on the F-16 before they are allowed to fly one on their own.

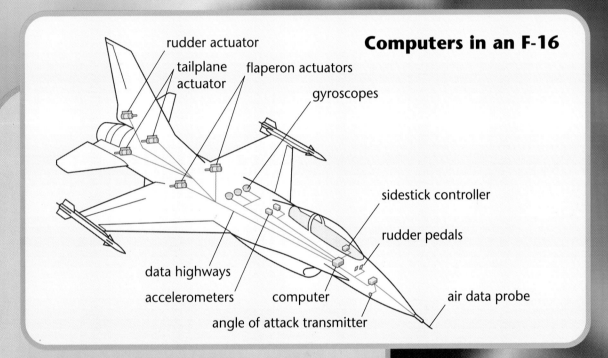

Computers in an F-16

- rudder actuator
- tailplane actuator
- flaperon actuators
- gyroscopes
- sidestick controller
- rudder pedals
- data highways
- accelerometers
- computer
- air data probe
- angle of attack transmitter

COMPUTERS IN CONTROL

The moving parts of a fly-by-wire fighter, such as the **rudder,** are moved by devices called actuators. The actuators are controlled by the airplane's computers. The computers need to know how much the airplane is turning, diving, or climbing, and in which direction, so that they can move the actuators by exactly the right amount. This information comes from devices called **accelerometers** and **gyroscopes.** They enable the computers to double-check

Lockheed F-16 Fighting Falcon

Type: fighter-bomber
Country: United States
Crew: 1
Wingspan: 32.8 ft (10.0 m)
Top speed: 1,320 mph (16,875 km/hr)
Max weight: 37,203 lb (16,875 kg)
Weapon load: 13,735 lb (6,230 kg)

SAFETY FIRST

Fighters cost millions of dollars each, but they can be replaced easily by building more. Fighter crews are much more important, and they take years to train. So, they need to be protected as much as possible.

Fighter designers must try to think of every danger the crews might face and then design airplanes to protect them. Some safety systems are built into airplanes. Others are built into the clothes that the crews wear, and even into their seats. Most of these safety systems work automatically because the crew may be unable to operate them. In an emergency, if a pilot or weapons officer has to escape from a fighter, there are systems to get him or her out of the airplane quickly and down to the ground safely.

GETTING AIR

The higher you go, the thinner the air gets. Fighters often fly thousands of feet above the ground. At that height, the air is too thin to breathe. Fighter pilots wear masks that supply them with **oxygen.** The mask also contains a microphone that is connected to the fighter's radio.

DRESSING FOR WORK

Fighter crews wear a special suit called a partial pressure suit, or G-suit. When a fighter turns sharply, the **G-force** pushes the blood down out of the pilot's head. If the brain doesn't receive enough blood, it is starved of oxygen and the pilot blacks out. The G-suit prevents this by squeezing the legs, which keeps blood from draining into them. F-15 and F-16 pilots also wear a special mask to help them breathe. In tight turns, the pilot breathes high-pressure air. At the same time, a vest inflates to balance the pressure on the outside of the chest.

STAYING AFLOAT

All fighter pilots wear a life preserver. If a pilot has to parachute into the sea, the life preserver automatically inflates and keeps the pilot afloat. The pilot may land unconscious, so it's vital that the life preserver turns him or her onto the back to keep his or her face out of the water.

ROCKET SEATS

If a fighter is about to crash, the crew has no choice but to get out of the airplane. Each crew member sits in a special seat called an ejector seat. To eject, he or she pulls a handle. A rocket in the seat fires, blasting it clear of the airplane. The crew member is out of the airplane within half a second and floats to the ground by parachute.

FAST AND FURIOUS

The designers who create fighters and attack airplanes for air forces and navies have produced some amazing machines.

Every time a new fighter or attack airplane is built, other air forces and navies around the world study it. If they think their own airplanes or ground defenses can't defeat it, they may develop a new airplane of their own. It is a long process. For example, from the time the United States decided to build the F-22 until it enters service, the whole design and testing process will have taken 25 years. The cost, in both money and effort, is enormous. But no matter who designs the planes, they have to come up with their own unique solutions to design problems.

SU-27 FLANKER

The Russian Sukhoi Su-27 is one of the world's best fighters. When it first appeared in air displays, its abilities astonished everyone. A move called the cobra is very popular. The fighter flies normally, then the nose suddenly tips up until the airplane is standing on its tail, still flying forward. Then the nose falls forward again, and the airplane flies on. It is called the cobra because it looks like a cobra snake raising its head.

TANK-BUSTER

Not all attack fighters have to be super fast. The top speed of the American A-10 Thunderbolt II is only 435 mph (700 kph), but speed is not important. The A-10 is designed to fly close to the ground and attack tanks and other armored vehicles. Because it flies so low and slow, it is designed to survive a lot of damage. It can fly home even if one engine is entirely destroyed. The pilot sits in a section armored for protection against attack from below.

Smoke pours from an A-10 Thunderbolt as the pilot fires the big seven-barreled tank-busting gun in the plane's nose.

A-10 Thunderbolt II

Type: anti-armor close support attack airplane
Country: United States
Crew: 1
Wingspan: 57.4 ft (17.5 m)
Top speed: 435 mph (700 km/hr)
Max weight: 50,001 lb (22,680 kg)
Weapon load: 15,984 lb (7,250 kg)

FUTURE FIGHTER

The next U. S. attack aircraft is already being designed. At first, it was called the Joint Strike Fighter. When Lockheed Martin was chosen to build it, it became known as the F-35. While the F-22 concentrates on **combat** with other aircraft, the F-35 will attack ground targets. There will be three versions of the aircraft. The air force will fly the standard version. The navy version will have bigger wings and a stronger structure for landing on a carrier deck. The **Marine Corps** version will be a short takeoff and vertical landing (STOVL) aircraft.

DATA FILES

The main fighters in service with armed forces all over the world are listed below.

Attack fighter	Place of origin	Wingspan	Top speed	Max weight	Weapon load
A-10 Thunderbolt II anti-armor close-support attack airplane	United States	57.4 feet 17.5 meters	435 mph 700 km/hr	50,001 lb 22,680 kg	15,984 lb 7,250 kg
Eurofighter EFA2000 multirole fighter	Europe	34.5 feet 10.5 meters	1,320 mph 2,125 km/hr	46,297 lb 21,000 kg	14,330 lb 6,500 kg
F-14 Tomcat navy interceptor/fighter-bomber	United States	64.0 feet 19.5 meters	1,555 mph 2,500 km/hr	70,768 lb 32,100 kg	14,506 lb 6,580 kg
F-15E Strike Eagle strike fighter-bomber	United States	43.0 feet 13.1 meters	1,650 mph 2,655 km/hr	80,997 lb 36,740 kg	24,493 lb 11,110 kg
F-16 Fighting Falcon fighter-bomber	United States	32.8 feet 10.0 meters	1,320 mph 2,125 km/hr	37,203 lb 16,875 kg	13,735 lb 6,230 kg
F/A-18 Hornet fighter-bomber	United States	40.4 feet 12.3 meters	1,190 mph 1,915 km/hr	51897 lb 23,540 kg	15,499 lb 7,030 kg
F-22 Raptor advanced tactical fighter	United States	44.3 feet 13.5 meters	$1,245^+$ mph $2,000^+$ km/hr	59,999 lb 27,215 kg	classified
F-117 Nighthawk stealth attack aircraft	United States	43.3 feet 13.2 meters	610 mph 980 km/hr	52,503 lb 23,815 kg	5,005 lb 2,270 kg
Gripen JAS 39 multirole fighter	Sweden	26.3 feet 8.0 meters	1,320 mph 2,125 km/hr	27,503 lb 12,475 kg	14,330 lb 6,500 kg
Harrier II STOVL close-support aircraft	UK/U.S.	30.5 feet 9.3 meters	660 mph 1,065 km/hr	30,997 lb 14,060 kg	13,228 lb 6,000 kg
MiG-25 Foxbat interceptor	Russia	46.3 feet 14.1 meters	2,110 mph 3,395 km/hr	90,390 lb 41,000 kg	8,819 lb 4,000 kg
Rafale multirole fighter	France	35.8 feet 10.9 meters	1,320 mph 2,125 km/hr	54,013 lb 24,500 kg	13,228 lb 6,000 kg
Sukhoi Su-27 Flanker multirole fighter	Russia	48.2 feet 14.7 meters	1,555 mph 2,500 km/hr	66,139 lb 30,000 kg	17,637 lb 8,000 kg
Tornado IDS interdictor strike aircraft	Europe	45.6 feet 13.9 meters	920 mph 1,480 km/hr	61,619 lb 27,950 kg	19,842 lb 9,000 kg

Attack fighters have advanced a great deal since the days of this British Sopwith Camel fighter used during World War I (1914–1918).

FURTHER READING

Berliner, Don. *Stealth Fighters and Bombers*. Berkeley Heights, N. J.: Enslow Publishers, 2001.

Chant, Christopher. *Role of the Fighters and Bombers*. Broomall, Penn.: Chelsea House Publishers, 1999.

Gunston, Bill. *Fighter Planes*. Hauppage, N.Y.: Barron's Educational Series, 1999.

Masters, Nancy Robinson. *Fighter Planes of World War II*. Danbury, Conn.: Scholastic Library Publishing, 2000.

Miller, Ron. *A Century of Flight: The History of Aviation*. Las Vegas, Nev.: American Institute for Education, 1998.

Seidman, David. *F/A-18 Hornet*. New York, N.Y.: Rosen Publishing Group, 2002.

An older reader can help you read these books:

Beyer, Julie. *Jet Figher: The Harrier AV-8B*. Danbury, Conn.: Scholastic Library Publishing, 2000.

Reavis, Tracey. *Stealth Jet Fighter: The F-117A*. Danbury, Conn.: Scholastic Library Publishing, 2000.

By the 1940s, fighters such as this American P-51 Mustang could fly at speeds of up to 373 mph (600 km/hr).

GLOSSARY

accelerometer device that measures acceleration

aileron moving part of a fighter's wings. When one aileron tilts up and the other tilts down, the airplane rolls.

airframe body of an aircraft without its engines

air-superiority fighter fighter designed to seek out enemy planes and clear them from the sky. This means that troops can move around freely on the ground without suffering air attacks.

catapult equipment fitted to an aircraft carrier to launch combat airplanes along the deck

cockpit part of an aircraft where the pilot sits. Some fighters have a second cockpit where a weapons officer sits.

combat fighting

control surface part of an airplane's wings and tail that is moved by the pilot to steer the airplane

disperse to scatter something over a wide area

dogfight close combat between fighters chasing each other through the sky

elevator moving part of a fighter's tail. Elevators change an airplane's pitch. When the elevators tilt up or down, the airplane climbs or dives.

exhaust hot gases that rush out of an engine

fuselage body of an airplane. A fighter's fuselage contains the engine, or engines, and the cockpit.

G-force force equal to one or more times the force of gravity

gyroscope device made from a spinning disk. When an airplane turns or tilts, gyroscopes inside it stay in the same position. This enables computers to keep track of an airplane's movements.

interceptor type of fighter designed to stop the approach of enemy fighters or bombers

jet engine type of engine that produces a high-speed jet of gas to thrust an aircraft forward

lift force, acting upward, that is produced by an airplane's wings or a helicopter's rotor blades as they cut through the air

Mach aircraft's speed divided by the speed of sound. Mach 1 is the speed of sound. Mach 2 is twice the speed of sound.

maneuverable/maneuverability ability to turn this way and that with ease

Marine Corps branch of the U.S. armed forces composed of seagoing troops

nosewheel plane's landing wheel underneath its nose

oxygen one of the gases that make up air

radar Radio Detection and Ranging, a method for finding distant objects by sending out radio waves and picking up the reflections that bounce back

round single bullet, artillery shell, or tank shell

rudder part of a fighter's tail fin that swivels to the left and right to turn the airplane's nose left or right. Turning to the left and right is also called yaw.

simulation copy of a problem or situation created inside a computer. A whole aircraft can be created, or modeled, in a computer. It can then be tested to see how the real airplane will fly in different conditions and at different speeds.

stick short term for *control stick* or *joystick,* the main flying control in a small aircraft's cockpit. Moving the stick in any direction makes the plane tilt in that way.

supersonic faster than the speed of sound

tail fin part of an aircraft that stands up at the rear end. It keeps the plane's tail steady and stops it from swinging from side to side.

tailplane small, winglike part on either side of an airplane's tail

taxies when an aircraft moves along the ground under its own power

thrust force produced by an engine to propel an aircraft

titanium strong, lightweight metal that withstands very high temperatures and doesn't rust. Titanium is often used to make parts of the fastest airplanes.

turbine part of a jet engine that is spun by the jet of gas rushing out of the engine. The spinning turbine drives the engine's fan and compressor.

variable geometry describes a plane that can make its wings stick straight out from the side for flying slowly and then swing them back to form a slender dartlike shape for flying fast. It is also called swing-wing.

Western concerning North American and West European countries

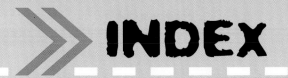

INDEX

A-10 Thunderbolt II 27, 28
accelerometers 23
actuators 23
afterburners 17
ailerons 7
AIM-7 Sparrows 4
AIM-9 Sidewinders 4
AIM-120 AMRAAMs (Advanced Medium-Range Air-to-Air Missiles) 4
air-superiority fighters 4, 6
air-to-air combat 4, 6, 7, 27
aircraft carriers 18, 19
avionics (aviation electronics) 13

cannon 4
cockpit 5, 9, 10, 12, 13, 14, 23
composites 12
computers
    flight computers 13, 22, 23
    simulations 10

design 5, 6–7, 24, 26, 27
dogfights 6

ejector seats 25
elevators 7
elevons 7
Eurofighter 6, 17, 28

F-14 Tomcat 18, 19, 28
F-15 Eagle 4–5
F-15E Strike Eagle 4, 5, 28
F-16 Fighting Falcon 22, 23, 28
F/A-18 Hornet 18, 19, 28
F-22 Raptor 10–15, 17, 26, 28
F-35 27
F-117 Nighthawk 8–9, 28
fighter-bomber 5, 14, 18,

flaperons 7
fly-by-wire 22–23
fuselage 10

G-force 22, 25
G-suits 25
Gripen 7, 28
ground targets 4, 7, 27
gyroscopes 23

Harrier 20, 21, 28
Head-Up Display (HUD) 13

information, sorting and communicating 14
interceptors 4, 6
    supersonic interceptors 14, 18

jet engines 9, 12, 16–17, 21
jump jets 20–21

life preservers 25
low flying 8, 27

Mach numbers 14, 15
maneuverability 4, 10, 11, 22,
manufacturing 12
materials 12
MiG-25 6, 28
MiG-31 6
missiles 4

navy fighters 18–19, 27

oxygen masks 24

pilots and crew 5, 14, 15, 22, 23, 24–25, 27
pressurized breathing system 25
prototypes 11

radar 8, 9, 10
Rafale 6, 28
reconnaissance 7
refueling 5
rudder 7, 23

safety 24–25
short take-off and vertical landing (STOVL) 20, 27
Sopwith Camel 28
speed 4, 6, 14, 27
speed of sound 6, 14, 15
stealth airplanes 8–9
steering 7, 21, 22
stick 5, 22
Sukhoi Su-27 26, 28
supercruise 17

tail fin 7, 11
tailplanes 7
tailerons 7
terrain masking 8
test flights 11
titanium 12
turbines 16

vectored thrust 11, 15
vertical takeoff 20, 21
virtual product development 10

weapons 4, 9
wings 10, 14
    delta shape 19
    folding wings 19
    swing-wing design 18, 19